A

'FAILED-AGAIN'

CHRISTIAN

Kintsugi is the Japanese art of repairing broken porcelain with melted gold. In many cases, the restored piece is even more beautiful and valuable than the original. This is an apt metaphor for the followers of Jesus whose broken lives have been restored with great love and care. *We have this treasure in jars of clay…*

A 'Failed-Again' Christian

Explaining Why I Believe

Edited by Ben Leon Tan

Published by BLT Productions

ISBN: 9798316382484

By the same author

Lost Heritage
Sting in the Tail (Mandarin, Farsi)
Jubilee Gospel (German, Mandarin, Bahasa Indonesia)
Fighting Poverty through Enterprise (German, Bahasa Indonesia)
Social Impact Investing: New
Agenda in Fighting Poverty
Jubilee and Social Justice
Understanding The Bible Through Eastern Eyes

Contents

A 'FAILED-AGAIN' CHRISTIAN

Introduction

'Science without religion is lame, religion without science is blind' –
Albert Einstein

I am sometimes asked "What kind of Christian are you?" My
standard answer is that I am a 'failed-again' Christian, as opposed
to the 'born-again' type. I say "failed-again" because, for me, the
Christian faith is for those who realise they are imperfect, who
need a second, third, or fourth chance and who fail to live up to
their own high standards of behaviour. That's me. I have failed to
consistently live up to these standards – as a husband, father,
brother and neighbour. And with each failure I've needed the grace
of forgiveness. I am also hesitant to use the term "born-again"
because the current brand of arrogant, triumphalist, money-fuelled
Christianity that has become associated with it, is a far cry from the
faith of the carpenter from Nazareth. At the risk of upsetting some
people, there is a huge difference between Christianity and
'*Churchianity*'.

This is the story of my personal journey of faith – from growing up
in a Taoist family in predominantly-Muslim Malaysia, to becoming
a half-baked 'Darwinist,' to this next stage of my journey as a
follower of Jesus. As a bit of an egghead and a failed scientist, I
have always needed evidence for my beliefs. Therefore, my journey
had to involve rational explanations for God, creation, miracles,
and the like. For me, faith cannot be an irrational leap in the dark.
In this book, I explore the evidence I have gathered – using nature,
science, and even the strange worlds of quantum physics,
chemistry, and biology – to explain how I have arrived at this
juncture of my faith. There will be no mathematical proofs or slam-

dunks, only plausible explanations and ideas that pointed me towards Christianity. If anything, readers will hear my self-doubts between the lines.

There's no particular order in which you must read this book. Feel free to jump straight to the issue that gives you the most angst and begin there. Welcome to exploring these issues in these pages with me. May we humbly seek truths that will give purpose to our lives.

'How little we know. How eager to learn.'
– Sir John Templeton, renowned investor and philanthropist

Hypocrites And Simpletons

Christians are variously viewed as both hypocrites and simpletons. They are hypocrites because they preach one thing but live another, and they are simpletons because they believe in miracles and the Bible (hasn't science contradicted the Bible?). These two issues, along with the question of suffering, were my major objections to becoming a Christian.

Let us deal first with the accusation of hypocrisy. I love a sign I saw outside a church once which said: "The church is full of hypocrites, but there is room for one more!" Being a Christian doesn't mean that you are better than anybody. In fact, Christianity actually teaches the opposite, that we are all likely worse than we think we are. Frankly, if you knew the worst about me, you would not want to be my friend. That's why the type of finger-pointing, moralising, condemning caricature we see in the media has no place in true Christianity. The fact that Christians can't live up to their own standard doesn't disprove the validity of the standard. Yes hypocrites - guilty as charged.

I became a Christian, despite what I knew of the church. Like many people, I was put off by what I saw as a place of rules, strange practices, and judgemental pharisees. I wanted to be a follower of Jesus, not a member of the commercial religious complex. It is to the collective shame of the church that it has been exposed for so many indefensible moral issues - be it infidelity, abuse of power, greed, racism, slavery or the paedophile scandals. What I've come to realise though is that the church isn't full of good people, but rather people who want to be good. The goal of a Christian has never been about perfection, an impossible ideal, but rather is about being gradually transformed to live better, more purposeful lives. The church is a hospital and rehab centre for sinners, not a museum for saints. A friend of mine describes it as a place for scumbags in rehab. But God is a Kintsugi expert. He is able to put broken lives together and turn them into people with even greater inner beauty.

As for the accusation of being scientifically-naive simpletons: episodes such as Galileo's struggles with the Catholic church[1] over the heliocentric model of the universe and the 1860 Huxley-Wilberforce debate[2] on evolution in Oxford are regularly trotted out as exemplars of the antagonistic relationship between faith and science. Certainly, early in my student days, I was led to believe that no self-respecting scientist could possibly believe in God or the Bible. Yet, the deeper I dug into science, the more I discovered that some of the greatest scientists, both living today and throughout history, have been theists. Gregor Mendel, Blaise Pascal, Sir Isaac Newton, Georges Cuvier, Louis Pasteur, Lord Kelvin, James Maxwell, Max Planck, Francis Collins - all of them believed in God.[3] Even the most famous scientist of them all, Albert Einstein, rejected the premise that science and religion must be in conflict with one another.

---

[1] An interesting article in Scientific American about Galileo's struggle with the church: https://www.scientificamerican.com/blog/observations/did-galileo-truly-say-and-yet-it-moves-a-modern-detective-story/

[2] For a good explanation of this debate, see: https://oumnh.ox.ac.uk/great-debate

[3] Gregor Mendel was the father of genetics. Blaise Pascal laid the foundations for the modern theory of probabilities. Sir Isaac Newton discovered Newton's laws, or 'falling apples' to you and me. Georges Cuvier was the father of comparative anatomy and palaeontology. Louis Pasteur was the father of microbiology and Pasteur Institute fame. Lord Kelvin laid the foundation for modern physics. James Maxwell ranked with Isaac Newton and Albert Einstein for his scientific contribution to physics. Max Planck was the originator of quantum theory. Albert Einstein is too famous to need an introduction. Finally, Francis Collins headed up the Human Genome Project that sequenced the entire human genome.

A few fascinating cases-in-point are Michael Faraday, Georges Lemaitre, and Charles Darwin. In the 19th century, Michael Faraday revolutionised both physics and chemistry by originating the concept of the electromagnetic field and discovering benzene, the principles of electromagnetic induction, and the laws of electrolysis. He was also a devout Christian who served as a deacon and an elder in his local church. He believed that nature and the Bible had the same author and thus he said, "The natural works of God can never by any possibility come into contradiction with the higher things that belong to our future existence." Georges Lemaitre, who first proposed the Big Bang, was likewise a devoted Christian who saw no conflict between science and faith. In fact, he was both a Catholic priest and a professor of physics at the Catholic University of Louvain when, in 1931, he proposed in an academic paper that the expanding universe must have originated at a finite point in time. His religious interests were as important to him as his science, and he served as the president of the Pontifical Academy of Sciences from 1960 until his death. Even Charles Darwin himself, who could be said to have sparked the most fervent round of the religion vs. science debate, rejected that his theory of natural selection was necessarily at odds with theism. Darwin had trained as an Anglican priest and, in his diaries from his years sailing aboard the Beagle, even referred to himself as "quite orthodox." Though his personal religious convictions oscillated throughout his life, in 1879 he wrote to a friend saying, "It seems to me absurd to doubt that a man may be an ardent Theist & an evolutionist...What my own views may be is a question of no consequence to any one except myself...In my most extreme fluctuations I have never been an atheist in the sense of denying the existence of a God."[1]

---

[1] https://www.darwinproject.ac.uk/letter/?docId=letters/DCP-LETT-12041.xml

Later on, we will address more fully the question of whether the Bible and science contradict each other. For now, it suffices to say that for these great scientists, science and faith were not irreconcilable.

Can You Trust The Bible?

The most common question about the trustworthiness of the Bible is whether we can take the Bible literally. The answer to that question is both Yes and No. Just like we do today, the Bible uses figurative speech. When I say to my wife, "Darling, would you be an angel and please make me a cup of tea?" I do not intend for her to literally become an angel. However, I do intend for her to make me a cup of tea. Likewise, when I say that my sons are cheeky monkeys, I am not saying we live in a zoo, but I am saying that they possess qualities reminiscent of monkeys. The Bible uses everyday language in this same way. For example, the Bible talks about the sun rising in the East and setting in the West, just like we all do in normal speech. Now, everyone knows that, scientifically, these statements are nonsense. The sun doesn't "rise" or "set" at all, but rather the earth rotates. However, when we talk about the sunrise or sunset we aren't ignoring or rejecting scientific reality, we are just using everyday figurative speech. Similarly, the Bible speaks about 'the four corners of the earth' which some have taken hyper-literally to mean that the Bible supports the belief in a flat-earth.

Science uses language the same way. Scientists use models to explain observations that cannot be seen with the naked eye. So electrons are described as negatively charged particles 'orbiting' around a nucleus just like planets orbit the sun. But the atom isn't really a miniature solar system. Models are really metaphors that allow us to explain the properties and behaviour of atoms by using what is visible to explain what is invisible to both the naked eye and even the most powerful electron microscope. Therefore, models have their limitations and cannot be taken literally. Likewise in Christianity, we use the visible to help us understand the invisible and the models or metaphors used have their limitations and cannot be taken literally.

Jewish rabbis never interpreted the Genesis account of creation literally, the way that some Christian fundamentalists insist on doing today. When confronted with such literalists, I sometimes ask where are the one-eyed and one-handed Christians? After all, the Bible does say that if your eye causes you to sin you should pluck it out and if your hand causes you to sin you should chop it off! Or do they take literally Jesus' instruction to 'go sell all of your possessions, give the money to the poor, and come follow me?' No one seems to follow those parts of the Bible literally. No, rather than "literally," we need to read the Bible "literarily," meaning with all of the context, idioms, and metaphors that people use in their everyday speech.

 Understanding that the Bible uses figurative language helps us also to understand that Genesis, the first book of the Bible, was not written to be a scientific textbook. Its account of creation was written for ordinary people using everyday speech. In fact, in the original language, it is actually written in poetic form. How can we expect a few hundred words of poetry to accurately describe the whole creation process? Yet, that is the demand that many people try to place on it. If the author of Genesis had written the account of creation to spell out all of the scientific details, none of us would not be able to understand it!

Instead of a textbook, these first chapters of the Bible were meant to express the essential truth that the universe was created by choice, not by chance. There is a Creator behind it all and he made the world out of nothing. These chapters also tell us that he created the world in stages, not all at once. There were periods in between each important stage, almost as if, like all artists, God sat back to admire his handiwork. The Bible tells us neither the details of how the Creator created the universe nor how long he took doing it. Anyone who claims to see further technicalities than those is misreading the intended purpose of the text and misrepresenting the teachings of Christianity.

When we read the Bible, we need to not only respect the author's use of language but also the genre of each book. Just as we change our expectations depending on whether we are reading a history book versus a play versus a law document, so too should our reading of the Bible shift as it switches genres. The Bible includes many different genres: history, songs, poetry, prophecy, letters, parables, and more. We should be very wary about making either theology or science out of poetry. For example, the Psalms are a collection of songs encompassing all of humankind's experiences – joy, fear, sadness, depression, rejection, relief. While some understanding of human nature and psychology can be gained from them, they are what they are – songs. We should not go to them for scientific understanding, even though themes like creation can be found in them.

Can You Trust Science?

Before we discuss whether science is trustworthy, we need to distinguish between serious science and popular or layman science. All sorts of predatory companies make false or dangerous claims using a thin veneer of "science" to justify their practices. For example, serious scientific studies have shown no health benefits from large doses of vitamins, antioxidants, and supplements. Yet, popular science has caused these to become huge industries. Unfortunately, there is plenty of bad popular science floating around, from both atheists and Christians.

So now that we have disregarded the type of bogus "science" peddled by popular science, can we trust real science? Again, my answer is both Yes and No. We need to recognise the truths of science while still acknowledging that it is both constantly in flux and limited in its explanatory power. New scientific evidence is emerging all the time, and so while scientific truth is exact in its specificity, it is also incomplete. Our scientific knowledge and theories necessarily change when presented with evidence from new discoveries.

There are also limits to science's ability to answer fundamental questions about meaning, value, and beauty. Science excels at dismantling nature to discover the underlying laws and show how things work. However, science is completely helpless at showing why things are or what they mean. The limits of science is well stated by Stephen Hawking, the author of A Brief History of Time: "Although science may solve the problem of how the universe began, it cannot answer the question: why does the universe bother to exist? I don't know the answer to that."[1] Likewise, science can describe the refraction of light that causes a rainbow, but can't explain its beauty.

John Lennox, Emeritus Professor of Mathematics at the University of Oxford, poses yet another limitation – can we even trust the human mind to understand science? He writes, "If the atheists are right, that the mind that does science... is the end product of a mindless unguided process. Now, if you knew your computer was the product of a mindless unguided process, you wouldn't trust it. So, to me atheism undermines the rationality I need to do science." For Lennox, the evidence for cosmic design lies in the fundamental laws and structure of the universe; the rationality and intelligibility of the human mind and consciousness are pointers to the universe being created by design. Albert Einstein made a similar point. He said, "the only thing incomprehensible about the universe is that it is comprehensible."

Science is based on observation, but often it relies on the existence of things that cannot be seen to explain things that can. The esoteric world of quantum physics deals with a realm of the universe – subatomic particles – which is invisible. Yet we know that atoms and subatomic particles exist because we see their effects and derive benefits from them everyday in the form of electricity. In fact, there are many realities that we cannot see. Radio waves are passing through you right now but you would never know it unless you turn on your radio. Magnetism, static electricity, and quarks cannot be directly observed – but their effects can. What is love? Can we see it? We can see the effects and result of love, but not love itself.

---

[1] Black Holes and Baby Universes, 1994.

Both science and faith seek to develop coherent theoretical frameworks that fit the evidence. Science gathers evidence from experiments, observations, mathematical calculations, etc. and uses it to understand the natural world. Christianity follows that up by providing a framework for understanding what science can't explain, such as the regularity and intelligibility of the world, the meaning of life, suffering, and the improbable rise of a faith led by a penniless carpenter from the back waters of the Roman Empire.

Science deals with the question How, whereas faith deals with the question Why. Science may one day be able to tell us exactly how the universe started but it will not be able to tell us why or by whom it was started. A scientific analysis of my house will show how the house was built: timber-frame construction with seasoned Welsh oak beams and oak flooring from recycled French railway carriages, and so on. At one level, all this is very interesting, especially if you are an architect, builder, or interior designer. However, what is really interesting, and what scientific inquiry cannot determine, is to know who built it and why it was built in this way. I know the answer because I know the builder personally and I know why he built it. That's the difference between science and faith. They are not contradictory but complementary. I can say that I built a private cancer hospital in Malaysia in the 1980's. That only tells you the who and the why. It does not say anything about HOW it was built, with what materials, depth of foundation, and so on. In the same way, the Bible says that God created the world. It does not say how.

I think Christianity is a reasoned faith that requires us to use our minds as well as our hearts. I have come to believe that what we know about science, life, and human nature is consistent with the theory of a creator God.

Doesn't Science Contradict The Bible?

The prevalent misconception is that the old-fashioned ideas about creation found in Genesis have been contradicted by modern theories of evolution and that, because of this, every other part of the Bible must also be wrong. To address this, we need to understand what kind of a book the Bible is. The Bible is not a science textbook. It was written for ancient peasants in ordinary, everyday language, not for scientists in scientific language. We should not try, therefore, to extract scientific facts from it. It is a book that seeks to explain the who and the why behind the universe, not the hows. In that way, it is the perfect complement to science, not a contradiction.

Despite this caveat, as I look at the Genesis account, I arrive at the following observations:

1. Genesis tells us that the universe came into being in stages. God could have created it all in one go, but he didn't. Like all great artists, he created it a bit at a time, stepped back to enjoy it, saw that it was good, and went back later to do some more. This process actually sounds strangely similar to evolutionary theories that assert that life evolved gradually over millions of years. The French scientist Jean-Baptist Lamarck suggested that new species suddenly evolved whereas Darwin believed that the evolutionary process was more gradual. According to Lamarck, if new species suddenly 'appeared' there would not be any need for 'missing links' between the species. The absence of finding any serious contenders for the 'missing links' is causing some scientists to re-evaluate whether Lamarck's

theory might be preferable to Darwin's. Whichever of these theories are correct, science and Christianity agree that the universe came into being in stages, rather than as one instantaneous event. Likewise, both Genesis and Darwin agree that animal life, especially human, was the last to come into existence.

2. The world was not created in six 24-hour days. The word 'day' can mean a 24-hour period or it can mean an era, epoch, or age. Nowhere does the Bible state that the world is around 4500 years old. It does not ask us to believe in a 'young earth.' For thousands of years, Jewish scholars understood the word 'day' as an epoch. The Biblical account is not a textbook seeking to impart scientific knowledge because a precise knowledge of the age of the earth will not make us any wiser about how we should live our lives. I believe that the universe is very old because it takes millions of years for the light from the furthest stars to reach the earth. When we look up at the stars at night, we are seeing light that has already travelled millions of years before reaching us. I personally do not see any contradiction between science and Christianity here.

3. Genesis also tells us that the universe had a beginning. Most scientists also believe that the universe had a beginning. The current reigning theory for how the universe began is called the Big Bang. Basically, the theory states that a colossal explosion created all the matter we see in the universe, including the orderly solar system of planets and stars. I have some questions about this theory. In all other contexts, explosions always result in chaos, never order. So it's unlikely that a Big Bang could have resulted in the amazing order of the planets' orbits or the

rhythm of the earth's rotation. However, science does not currently have a better explanation for the origin of the universe. This theory however still begs the question: what caused the Big Bang? The Bible does not tell us whether or not the Big Bang actually happened. However, It does tell us that God was ultimately responsible for bringing the universe into being. That could have been through the mechanism of the Big Bang or through some yet-to-be-discovered process. Again, science and Christianity are not at odds.

4. This universe did not come about by chance, but by design. It didn't just happen. Someone, whom we call God the creator, put it there. That best explains the purpose and order we see both on earth and throughout the universe. Christians, therefore, disagree on this point with atheists who believe that by random chance the world exploded into existence. If this was true, the universe, and therefore life itself, would have no purpose or meaning.

5. When God created the universe, he said it was good. He is a good God who makes good things! This, of course, begs the question: where does all the evil we see around us come from? We will deal with this in a few more pages.

So, certain general realities about the universe can be known from the Genesis account of creation and most of these are in agreement with contemporary science. In fact, there are really only two major places where the Bible's account is at odds with science. The first is that there is a Creator behind the design of the universe rather than an unguided process of chance. The second is that the universe was objectively moral and good when it was first created, rather than neutral.

Well, what about evolution? Don't the similarities between the genes of the various species prove that evolution is true? After all, we share 98.4% of our DNA with chimpanzees. True, but we also share 75% of our DNA with zebra-fish and 50% of our DNA with bananas. Some have concluded that we must be 98.4% chimpanzee and 50% banana! That is clearly nonsense. Rather, the similarities between the genes can best be accounted for with design. For example, the Mercedes 320 engine 'evolved' from the 230. It is 95% similar to the Mercedes 230. Many components and design concepts are similar. The parallels between the two engines aren't best explained by spontaneous evolution or chance. No, the engines are very similar because the same company designed them both. In the same way, I believe that the evolutionary process, as described by Darwin and others, is best explained by a designer. This belief is called evolutionary creationism.

There are still issues with our understanding of evolution as the process for the origin of life. There is the chicken and egg problem of which came first: proteins cannot be synthesised without DNA (or RNA), but you cannot make DNA without protein enzymes to make the DNA building blocks. So there are still huge gaps in our understanding of the science of the origin of life. My other minor beef with evolution is why we don't have longer arms so we can scratch our backs properly (like the chimpanzees) or four thumbs so we can text faster on our mobile phones!

As of today, I am an evolutionary creationist. It is more than possible that God used a process of evolution to develop organic life over millions of years. There is overwhelming evidence that the earth is around 4.5 billion years old. The universe is ancient just looking at how many light years are needed before light from the stars reach the earth. Given this length of time and the laws of physics, chemistry, and biology, it is possible to envision how organic life came about on earth. But it still requires a designer. So, for me, evolutionary creationism is the best explanation of the evidence, for now anyway.

The Goldilocks Universe

Each person believes something about the universe. Either you can believe that this universe and life came about by chance, or you can believe that it came about by choice, but both require faith. It takes as much faith to be an atheist as it does to be a theist. Both are convictions made as responses to evidence.

One of the pieces of evidence that I find the most compelling is the fine-tuning of the universe. Someone has suggested that the chances of the universe coming into being by chance through the Big Bang is equivalent to an explosion in a printing factory resulting in a bound copy of the Oxford English Dictionary. Or imagine discovering the terracotta soldiers in China, one of the greatest archaeological finds of the last century. How would one explain their existence? One explanation is that they came about by chance, a spontaneous explosion in a pottery factory resulting in thousands of these intricate figurines. The other, more plausible explanation is that they have been designed and made by someone. We may not know who designed and made them. We may not know exactly why they were made and assembled in the tomb, but we can be sure there was a design and purpose behind it all.

The same is true of the universe. When we see the incredible intricacy of the universe, and the exactly fine-tuned parameters that it requires, the evidence demands a purposeful mind, a creator, to be behind it all. Dr. Philip Goff from Durham University, in an interview about his 2023 book Why? The Purpose of the Universe, explained it well:

In terms of empirical science, I focus on the fine-tuning of physics for life, the surprising discovery of recent decades that for life to be possible, certain numbers in physics had to be – like Goldilocks' porridge – "just right." For example, if dark energy – the force that powers the expansion of the universe – had been a little bit stronger, no two particles would have ever met, meaning no stars, planets, or any type of structural complexity. But if it had been significantly weaker, the universe would have collapsed back onto itself in the first split second of the big bang. For life to be possible, the strength of the force had to fall in a certain, narrow range. This is just one example among many. Ultimately, we face a choice. Either it's just an incredible fluke that the numbers in our physics are right for life. Or the numbers in our physics are as they are because they are the right numbers for life; in other words, there is some kind of goal-directedness towards life at the fundamental level of reality.

Goff uses the example of dark energy, but there are many, many more factors that require perfectly calibrated values in order for both the universe and biological life to exist.[1] One of my favourite

---

[1] Christopher Reese, in his article "What Scientific Proof Do We Have That There is a God?, pointed out some other excellent examples of fine tuning:" •The Strength of Gravity: The strength of gravity is determined by the gravitational constant. If gravity were significantly stronger, stars would burn out much faster, leaving less time for life to develop. On the other hand, if gravity were much weaker, stars might not form at all, preventing the creation of essential elements for life.• The Cosmological Constant: This constant relates to the expansion speed of the universe. If it were just a little bit larger, the universe would have expanded too rapidly for galaxies and stars to form. Conversely, if it were smaller, the universe might have collapsed back on itself before life had a chance to emerge.• The

examples comes from the "triple-alpha process," via which carbon is created in the nuclear fusion of stars. During this process, the energy levels of helium-4, beryllium-8, carbon-12, and oxygen-16 all must be at extremely precise levels in order for carbon (a fundamental element of all lifeforms) to form without it all turning into oxygen instead.

Atheists like Sir Martin Rees, the Astronomer Royal for the British throne, prefer to believe that these Goldilocks values are just coincidences. Yet, in his 1990 book Cosmic Coincidences he writes about the triple-alpha process, "This combination of coincidences, just right for resonance in carbon-12, just wrong for oxygen-16, is indeed remarkable. There is no better evidence to support the argument that the universe has been designed for our benefit – tailor made for man." Seeing the fine-tuning of the universe and acknowledging that it is evidence for design, but yet refusing to believe in a designer is Sir Martin's prerogative, which I respect. For me, it is easier to believe that the beauty, magnificence, and complexity of the universe points to a Designer, not a mindless, unguided process.

Those unfamiliar with the evidence for the fine-tuning of the universe will sometimes claim that it's a concept held only by Christians or theists. Yet, scientists who claim no religious affiliation or who are openly agnostic or atheist also acknowledge this fact about the universe. For example, Fred Hoyle, an eminent physicist and agnostic, stated, "A commonsense interpretation of

Strong Nuclear Force: This force holds together the protons and neutrons in an atom's nucleus. If it were slightly weaker, protons and neutrons wouldn't stick together, making complex atoms impossible. Without complex atoms, the chemical diversity necessary for life wouldn't exist. If it were stronger, protons could potentially bind to each other more readily, which could lead to a universe without stable hydrogen, an essential element for life. • The Size and Distance of the Earth from the Sun: Earth's position in the solar system is in what scientists call the Goldilocks Zone, where it's not too hot and not too cold, allowing for liquid water to exist."

29

the facts suggests that a super intellect has monkeyed with physics as well as chemistry and biology, and there are no blind forces worth speaking about in nature."[1] In his book A Brief History of Time, the late Stephen Hawking wrote, "The remarkable fact is that the values of these numbers seem to have been very finely adjusted to make possible the development of life." Physicist P.C.W. Davies, also religiously unaffiliated, insists that "the entire universe is balanced on a knife-edge, and would be total chaos if any of the natural 'constants' were off even slightly."

I am fascinated by the story about the elegance of mathematical formulae in the discovery of antimatter. The English physicist Professor Paul Dirac predicted the existence of antimatter in 1928 based on mathematics. He was working on combining quantum mechanics with Einstein's theory of relativity when he formulated an equation that suggested the existence of particles with the same mass as electrons but with opposite charge. This theoretical prediction was finally confirmed in 1932 when the American physicist Carl Anderson discovered the positron, the antimatter counterpart of the electron. For Dirac, the ability to use mathematical formulae for such discoveries was startling. He wrote: "It seems to be one of the fundamental features of nature that fundamental laws are described in terms of mathematical theory of great beauty and power, needing quite a high standard of mathematics for one to understand it…One could perhaps describe the situation by saying that God is a mathematician of a very high order, and He used very advanced mathematics in constructing the universe'. Such 'advanced mathematics' shows an intentionality about the universe that is difficult to explain away as 'chance'. That's why we live in a rational (and mathematically elegant) world.

---

[1] "The Universe: Past and Present Reflections." Engineering and Science, 1981.

What Kind Of God Is He?

Now that we have explored some plausible evidence for the existence of God, we can ask: what kind of God is he? We do not have to look only at the Bible to find out what God is like. Just by looking at the world he has made we can learn a lot about him.

When I look at nature, I arrive at the following truths:

1. He is very powerful. Just look at the forces of nature: volcanic eruptions, tornadoes, earthquakes, tsunamis. In addition, from the world of nuclear energy, we know that incredible power is packed inside an atom, which is so tiny that it is invisible not only to the naked eye but also to the most powerful electron microscope. Yet, unfathomable energy and power is locked within that minuscule system. His powerfulness can also be seen in the sheer vastness of the solar system. Light travels at 180,000 miles per second, and the distance travelled by light in one year is called a light year. The furthest stars are several million light years away. That is mindbogglingly big!

2. He is very creative. Look at the variety of trees, flowers, insects, and animals around us. I had a friend called Harold who was a gardener. I have never met anyone as enthusiastic as him about the beauty of nature. He can point to the loveliness and variety of each blade of grass. We teach small children that no two snowflakes are identical, and that principle extends to nearly everything in our world. God has made man to be creative too – with our music, art, and technological innovations.

3. He is very orderly. He is not chaotic. Natural laws have been put in place to create an orderly and rational universe. The planets rotate in predefined orbits. The moon cycles through its phases every 29.5 days. Seasons come and go, right on schedule. Apples always fall downwards due to gravity. Even the human body is very orderly and delicately balanced. Too much or too little sugar in the blood leads to brain coma, and so the body has a system, insulin produced in the pancreas, to finely control the levels of sugar in the blood.

4. He is highly intelligent. Every time I step on a plane, my simple mind is baffled by how a few thousand tonnes of metal can hurtle through the air in defiance of gravity. Just look at the way all the planets are 'suspended' in space, orbiting around the sun and each other. How do you make whole planets suspend themselves in nothing but empty space? Is it dark matter? Simple questions like these ones reveal how limited our scientific understanding still is. Humankind can become very proud of what we have all figured out, but our knowledge is only a drop in the bucket when compared to everything we don't know. Therefore, it must take an amazingly intelligent engineer to plan and construct the entire universe. Thank goodness that when he made us, he infused us with a small portion of that intelligence and creativity. What a dull world it would have been without it.

5. He is personal. Why can we deduce that? Because human beings are personal and social creatures. We communicate and relate. We have personalities. God is like that too, only even more so. In fact, God has to be personal in order to have created us with personalities. We, however, must have

inferior personalities because all creators can only create something inferior to themselves, never something superior. A great example is the current craze for robotic pets with personality. We are trying to make robotic pets that are able to relate and respond to us, however they will always have limited personalities because we created them. It is the same between us and God. He is a personal God and wants to relate and communicate with us. Wow!

What Are Humans?

Our current society has two main views of human beings. The first is that humans are highly evolved animals, descended from apes. The Naked Ape by Desmond Morris takes this view and traces humans back to the jungle. As evolved animals, we may be sophisticated monkeys, but we sure can behave like wild animals. In fact, the brutality of the 20th Century – including the mass murder of the Holocaust, the genocides of Idi Amin's Uganda, and the barbarity of Pol Pot's Cambodia – show that people can be, at times, lower than animals. No other member of the animal kingdom kills its own species in these kinds of numbers, purely for the sake of killing. It is obvious that there is something fundamentally flawed in our character. It is hard to take the view that humans are basically good except in the sense of the quote: "People are basically good. It's only their behaviour that lets them down!"

The second common view is a materialistic view, in which people are seen as merely lumps of chemicals: carbon, nitrogen, sulphur, oxygen, iron, zinc, and so on. Undoubtedly, the human body, when subjected to scientific analysis, can be reduced to these basic elements. However, this reductionist view does not even come close to explaining our collective experience of what it means to be human. How can it explain love? Is a kiss really the 'approach of 2 lips with a mutual exchange of microbes and saliva?' How can it explain human ingenuity, creativity, emotions, personality, and even our capacity for brutality? When someone dies, we all instinctively sense that the real 'person' is gone. We may behave worse than animals, but we sure are more than just lumps of chemicals. Otherwise the ransom we should pay any kidnapper should be $50 – the going price of a humans-worth of common chemicals.

So if humans aren't only animals and collections of atoms, what are we? The Bible's view is that human beings have been made in the image or likeness of God. This explains our personalities, our genius, and our capacity to do good. We are each "Imago Dei" – made in the image of God himself. If we truly believe this – that every man and woman, regardless of their abilities, their race, their creed, their origins, or their individual idiosyncrasies, is made in the image of our Maker – then it means every human being has an intrinsic value. It also places upon us a non-negotiable duty to uphold the sanctity and the dignity of human life at every stage, from the womb to the tomb. It means we cannot say that someone is only of value if they are young, healthy, productive, and of course, good-looking. Even the feeble, old, sick, homeless, or unborn are made in the image of God.

The Bible also tells us that human beings, though wonderfully made in the image of God, have become infected by evil. Like a cancer, this evil is festering away and will eventually destroy us. All of us, therefore, contain a capacity for good as well as for wrong. This evil is what the Bible calls sin. Whenever this word is used, we immediately think of sexual misdemeanours. I guess this is because the church throughout history has highlighted this particular form of sin.

However, sin really means falling short of God's perfect standards, something we all do. I remember watching a debate once and hearing an atheist professor of humanities say, "Anyone who has young children will have no problems believing in original sin!" How true. Children can be angels as well as little monsters. At a young age, they can exhibit sweetness, wonder, and compassion one minute and then be stubborn, selfish, and amazingly cruel the next. Adults do the same: we can show politeness and respect to the bank teller and then berate our spouse the whole way home.

These two teachings of the Bible – that we are all made in the image of God and yet we all have been tainted by sin – make perfect sense of the human experience. An honest examination of both ourselves and everyone around us reveals that we do not truly live like we are just apes or bunches of chemicals. We naturally live and talk as if the Christian explanation is true. I believe that it rings the truest with our experience, not because we are misguided or delusional, but perhaps because it is true.

Why Suffering?

If a God exists and he made the whole world and created humans in his image, then it must be fun, living in God's world, right? Wrong. We have messed up the world pretty badly. Two world wars, numerous genocides, the destruction of the rain-forests, climate change, pollution of our environment, depressing inner-city ghettos, refugee camps, homeless children, and suicide bombers. The list goes on. Living on earth is like being invited to stay at Buckingham Palace whilst the Queen is away. Imagine trashing the palace and abusing all of its facilities. What would Her Majesty think when she returns? Similarly, we have been living in God's world but in our own way. We have not had the courtesy to respect his property and his laws. He has laid down laws about how we should steward the environment, behave towards each other, care for the elderly and the vulnerable. We are meant to love and not to murder. Incidentally, the Ten Commandments are all about respect – for God, property, relationships, and reputation.

So, where did all of this evil come from? Is there even such a thing as right and wrong, good and evil? When God created the universe, he said it was good. After all, he is a good God! It begs the question then, where does all the evil and suffering we see around us come from then? There is both a simple and a complex answer. The simple answer is that humankind was created with free will and our actions have consequences – both good and bad. If we were robots, controlled by someone or something, there would not be any suffering. The complex answer is simply that the issue of suffering is difficult for both theists and atheists.

The comedian Stephen Fry spoke for many when he described a hypothetical creator as "stupid" and an "utter maniac" for designing a world filled with suffering. On an Irish television program in 2015, Fry was asked by the host, Gay Byrne, what he would say to God if he arrived at the pearly gates of heaven. The actor and author replied:

> I think I'll say, 'bone cancer in children? What's that about? How dare you? How dare you create a world in which there is such misery that is not our fault? It's not right. It's utterly, utterly evil. Why should I respect a capricious, mean-minded, stupid god who creates a world that is so full of injustice and pain? That's what I'd say… The god who created this universe, if it was created by a god, is quite clearly a maniac, utter maniac, totally selfish. We have to spend our life on our knees thanking him? What kind of god would do that?

I respect Mr Fry's honesty and directness. That is how a lot of people view the problem of suffering. This is how I have grappled with this complex issue: I see suffering coming from two main sources, from both humans ourselves and from nature.

First, much of the suffering we see is actually caused by human beings. We suffer because of the self-centred behaviour of corrupt tyrants responsible for mass murders, misguided policies, and the plundering of their country's coffers. On a more individual level, we suffer because of bad, but common, human behaviours, like stealing, lying, selfishness, gossip, and cruelty. Or suffering may be caused by more sensational evil behaviour like drunk driving, murder, and suicide bombing. Suffering can be caused by human failure or negligence that causes an accident or the unintentional spreading of suffering, such as how human ignorance speeds the transmission of new diseases. It may be caused by our lifestyle choices, like how over-consumption causes obesity related diseases and contributes to the greenhouse effect, causing global warming and climate change. It may be the greed of corporations, causing pollution to rivers and forests resulting in toxic deaths, malformed babies, and depriving people of their livelihood. Further, some of the suffering we attribute to nature is actually human-caused. For example, droughts do not have to result in famine. Famines are ultimately caused by human incompetence, corruption, and a failure to allocate resources fairly and on-time. In all of these cases, humankind is responsible for the evil we see in the world, not God.

Second, suffering is caused by nature. The Bible states that God did a good job when he created the world. Everything was set up right and operated according to the natural laws he had put in place. Man and nature were supposed to live in perfect harmony. The picture we have is poetically described as one "where the lion shall eat grass and lie down with the lamb!" However when humankind became infected with evil, nature too became infected and the harmony was shattered. Because we were fighting God, nature started to fight with us. This is now an imperfect world populated by imperfect people operating on imperfect laws. Most of the time the natural laws work reasonably well otherwise we would not have existed this long. But now and again they don't. Where previously germs and viruses would live in harmony with human beings, some are now positively dangerous. Likewise, the natural laws of genetics have been corrupted so that the copying of genetic information is now not always accurate, leading to genetic abnormalities. These abnormalities lead to disease and shortened life spans, hence the bone cancer Stephen Fry mentioned. A benign world gave way to a hostile one in which we have to 'tame' nature

41

in order to survive. Natural disasters – volcanic eruptions, earthquakes and tsunamis, which are all the result of shifts in the earth's crusts and tectonic plates – happen because the natural laws are still in operation, except they are not working in harmony anymore.

Inside each of the human body's 30 trillion cells, there is a digital database encoded in some 3.1 billion letters of DNA base pairs. Two trillion of these cells divide everyday. Every time a cell divides, it must copy its entire genome – all 3.1 billion letters of it. It's not surprising that there are inevitably errors when copying DNA at this rate. These copying errors are called mutations and we all have them. We are all mutants – get used to it! Our brains are full of mistakes, tiny typos of our DNA. Fortunately, not all mutations create harm. Most mutations are repaired by the body and are not harmful. However, some genetic abnormalities at birth are caused by these copying errors, either because of natural mistakes in DNA replication or because of chemicals such as thalidomide (the birth defects caused by chemicals are thus man-induced suffering). Mutations of bacteria like E coli that should exist in harmony with man but are now turned against us. Cancers are mutations caused by chemicals, radiation, viruses, or genetic miscopying.

The body has mechanisms in place to repair and prevent such mutations, but these defence mechanisms are also not perfect anymore.[1]

---

[1] "DNA replication is a truly amazing biological phenomenon. Consider the countless number of times that your cells divide to make you who you are—not just during development, but even now, as a fully mature adult. Then consider that every time a human cell divides and its DNA replicates, it has to copy and transmit the exact same sequence of 3 billion nucleotides to its daughter cells. Finally, consider the fact that in life (literally), nothing is perfect. While most DNA replicates with fairly high fidelity, mistakes do happen, with polymerase enzymes sometimes inserting the wrong nucleotide or too many or too few nucleotides into a sequence. Fortunately, most of these mistakes are fixed

So the classic question of why does God 'allow' suffering becomes a little easier to understand. In the sense that he has given man free will to choose good as well as to choose evil, he has 'allowed' suffering. If God took away our free will and turned us into obedient robots, there would be no suffering. In so far as he created the natural laws, he has 'allowed' natural disasters to happen. Take away the natural laws and we would not have any natural disasters, but neither would we have a rational world as we know it. When an employee of a large multinational corporation acts in a negligent way which results in a major tragedy, like the explosions at Union Carbide in Bhopal or BP's oil spill in the Gulf of Mexico, the chairman of the company has a certain responsibility. The chairman of the corporation has to take overall responsibility for the actions and conduct of their employees, even if they are not personally and directly involved. God is implicated in a similar way in that he is the one ultimately in charge. However the people he is responsible for are imperfect and self-centred, and consequently, suffering will happen.

But isn't God supposed to be all powerful? Yes and No. Yes, in that God originally had all the power and still does. But No, in that he chose to surrender some of his power when he gave us free will. He still has all the power but he chooses not to exercise all his power. God is the chess Grandmaster. Every move and decision we make is from our own free will. However because he is the Grandmaster, he is confident that his plans will win out in the end despite our attempts to foil him.

---

through various DNA repair processes." Scientists have reported mutation rates as low as 1 mistake per 100 million (10^{-8}) to 1 billion (10^{-9}) nucleotides, mostly in bacteria, and as high as 1 mistake per 100 (10^{-2}) to 1,000 (10^{-3}) nucleotides, the latter in a group of error-prone polymerase genes in humans." Pray, L. (2008) DNA Replication and Causes of Mutation. Nature Education 1(1):214

So, ultimately, we can argue that man is responsible for ALL the suffering in the world. God can be said to 'allow' it because he gave us the freedom to choose – unfortunately we made the wrong choice and have been living with its consequences ever since.

When people argue that suffering condemns God himself as an evil despot, they usually are picturing God as sitting in his lofty tower, either wilfully ignoring the suffering of his creation, or maniacally delighting in it. However, the Bible shows us the very opposite. God also sees the suffering in the world as a major problem and he designed a divine solution. The moral cancer of sin that we have all been infected with will kill us. In order to save us, God has to rip this moral cancer right out of us. He has done this through Jesus, who died on behalf of our sin. Like a father sucking the snake venom from his child, Jesus drew all of our sin into himself. Just like the father who dies from the effect of the venom so that his child might live, Jesus died so that we might live. That's the Bible's explanation for why Jesus died on the cross. It was to remove the sting and sentence of death over humanity.

We live in a cause and effect universe. If you punch someone, the effect is a bloody nose. The proponents of chaos theory use the 'butterfly effect' to describe how small and apparently insignificant incidents can set in motion a chain of events with far reaching consequences: they say that the flap of a butterfly's wing can ultimately cause a storm on another continent. If the 'butterfly effect' is true in the physical world, what then are the effects of human words, actions, and behaviours? There are moral consequences to our behaviour and Jesus took the full effect of these on our behalf – one man taking the full impact of humanity's behaviour like the buffer stopping a train at the station.

I once heard a story, which might be apocryphal. A single mother in Brazil was caught stealing in a supermarket and was brought before a judge. She pleaded for leniency saying that she stole so that she could feed her children that day. The judge was deeply moved by her story of poverty but nevertheless found her guilty as required by the law. She had to pay a fine or be sent to prison. She didn't have the money to pay the fine and so she faced a short prison sentence. After the sentencing, the judge removed his gown, came down from the bench and paid the fine for her so that she could go free and return to look after her children. This is also the Bible's explanation for God, in the person of Jesus, paying the penalty on our behalf for all the terrible things we have done as individuals and as humanity.

Wrestling With Some Common Objections

In my journey towards Christianity, I have had to wrestle with some thorny topics. These are issues that come up time and time again as objections that many have towards faith: what about miracles, the trinity, the virgin birth, and the divinity and humanity of Jesus? In each case, I had to look at the evidence to see if there are any rational explanations for them. Below are some of the conclusions that I have come to and the explanations as to why.

Miracles

For me, miracles can be explained as natural events either sped up or occurring at a specific time in answer to prayer. Healing recorded in the Bible could be explained as the body's natural healing process sped up. It is a supernatural miracle only because of the compressed time of the healing or because it occurred timeously in response to prayer, not because of the healing itself. We see 'spontaneous' healing in our everyday life – recovering from a cold or flu, for instance. The human body has a wonderful healing system. Spontaneous remission from cancer is a well known phenomenon but continues to puzzle us scientists. Research will eventually discover the mechanisms whereby the body can heal itself. So a miraculous healing can be explained by stimulating and accelerating the healing system. We now know that entire new organs can be formed from a single stem cell; it just requires the stem cell to be stimulated and for the laws of biology to take over. Regenerative biology, working with stem cells, will one day be able to regrow organs and limbs. Because all of our genes are present in every cell of our body, every cell has the genes to grow into a heart, an eye, or a limb. We just haven't learnt how to activate these genes yet, but scientists will discover this in the years to come. The Gene-Creator would certainly know how to activate them. But miracles by definition are rare occurrences, when the natural laws are suspended momentarily. Were it not so, the physical world will become unpredictable.

The parting of the Red Sea could also be explained as a natural event that coincided with the time the Israelite slaves needed to cross over to escape the on-rushing Egyptian army. So, this miracle could also be explained as a supernaturally-orchestrated event, timed for the benefit of the Israelites, but using natural means, similar to the way God used natural laws in evolutionary creation.

In *The Parting of the Sea: How Volcanoes, Earthquakes, and Plagues Shaped the Exodus Story*, geologist Barbara J. Sivertsen speculated about a link between the eruption of the volcano in Santorini (c. 1600 BC) and the Exodus of the Israelites from Egypt in the Bible. The photo below shows the remaining cliff face of the Greek Santorini Island in the Mediterranean Sea. A large chuck of the island falling into the sea would have caused a tsunami in Egypt. Rather than crossing the Red Sea, a marshy area in northern Egypt known as the Reed Sea would have been alternately drained and flooded by tsunamis caused by the caldera collapse, and could have been crossed during the Exodus. This is a theory but it goes to show that miracles can be explained as naturally occurring events that occur timeously in answer to a need or prayer.

For an alternative explanation by scientists from the University of Leicester, UK, on the crossing of the Red Sea by Moses AND later by Napoleon (in 1789!) see the Appendix: **'Moses' Parting of the Red Sea May Not Have Been A Miracle After All'**

The Trinity

This is a tough one to explain. The word "trinity" does not occur in the Bible. Rather, the word "trinity," which derives from the Latin word Trinitas, was first used in the second century to describe how the early Christians, including Jesus, were monotheistic and yet also believed that God exists as three distinct persons. At first glance, the concept of the trinity seems both contrived and preposterous. How can something be both one thing and also three things at the same time? However, science has taught me that many *'trinitarian'* entities exist in nature. For example, the electrons inside of a nitrate molecule form three different arrangements and yet it remains a single molecule: NO_3. In chemistry, this is called *'resonance'* or *'mesomerism.'* Nitrate's resonance structures – it's three arrangements of electrons – are illustrated below:

Seeing this picture, you might assume that these are three optional arrangements for the electrons in a nitrate molecule, as if some nitrates happen to be in form A and some take form B. That is not the case. Neither is it that nitrate switches back and forth between these arrangements at different points of time. Rather, the truth is that all three structures contribute to the overall structure of nitrate at all points in time. It is three, in one. The same is true of the carbonate molecule, seen below. It exists in all three forms, or resonate structures, at the same time, and yet is one chemical entity: CO3.

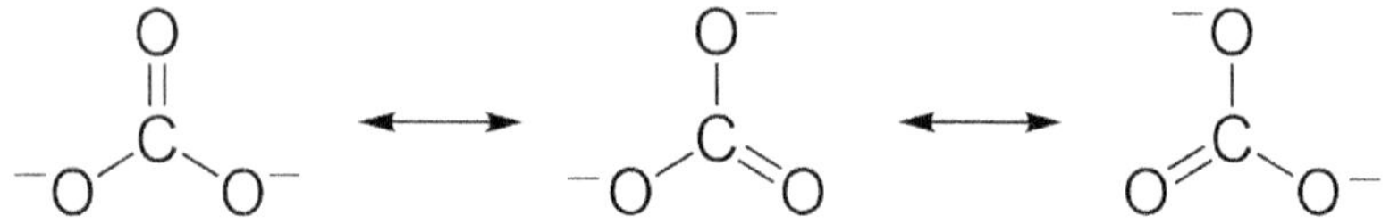

Another way of understanding how one entity can exist in various forms is the chemistry of isomers. Propanol has the formula C3H8O (or C3H7OH) and occurs as 3 isomers: propan-1-ol (n-propyl alcohol; I), propan-2-ol (isopropyl alcohol; II), and methoxyethane (ethyl-methyl-ether; III).

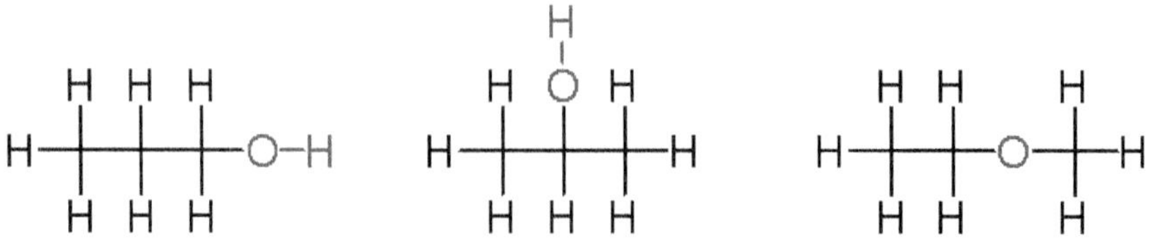

Interestingly, while all three isomers have the same chemical formula, and thus the same "substance," they have different structures and thus very different properties. Propan-1-ol and propan-2-ol are both colourless liquids used as ingredients in pharmaceuticals and household products like disinfectants. Methoxyethane, on the other hand, is an extremely flammable, colourless gas that causes dizziness and asphyxiation when inhaled.

Neither of these examples are a 'proof' for the Trinity, but rather an attempt to show that trinitarian states do exist in chemistry. By the way, the Hebrew word echad for 'one' can also mean 'unity' as in one grape or one bunch of grapes. The christian view of the Trinity is based on this understanding.

Virgin Birth

This is another tough one, but as we saw above with both the trinity and miracles, some form of this already exists in nature. Parthenogenesis (from the Greek parthenos meaning 'virgin' and genesis meaning 'creation') is a natural form of asexual reproduction in which growth and development of embryos occurs without fertilisation. In animals, parthenogenesis means the spontaneous development of an embryo from an unfertilised egg cell.

Parthenogenesis occurs naturally in some plants, some invertebrate animal species (including nematodes, water fleas, some scorpions, aphids, some mites, some bees, and parasitic wasps) and a few vertebrates (such as some fish, amphibians, reptiles). In parthenogenesis, the offspring are clones of the mother and hence are usually female. The embryo would have all gained all its chromosomes directly from the mother, including two XX chromosomes. In the particular case of aphids, parthenogenetically produced males and females are both clones of their mother, except that the males lack one of the X chromosomes (XO).

What was highly unusual in the case of THE virgin birth was that Jesus was a male. Perhaps it's a case similar to parthenogenesis with an XO? Again, none of this is 'proof' of the virgin birth, but only shows that virgin birth is a natural phenomenon in nature.[1]

The Divinity and Humanity of Jesus

Our understanding of light behaving as particles under certain conditions and as waves under others can give us an insight into this issue. The great Danish physicist Niels Bohr developed his concept of 'complementarity' and theoretical physicist Paul Dirac described his famous 'quantum field theory' to explain how both the wave and particle models offered a complementary description of the nature of light. Both are required to explain the complexity of the nature of light. The claims of Jesus as being both truly divine and truly human, 'two natures in one subject,' is analogous to Bohr's and Dirac's views on the complementarity of wave and particle models of light.

In the strange world of quantum physics, this duality of particles gets even more mysterious. Russian writer Stanyslav Kondrashov succinctly summarised some of the mind-bending truths of

---

[1] In his 2011 book Evolutionary Ecology, Eric R. Pianka points out an interesting case study. In 1956, women who believed they had had 'virgin births' were invited to volunteer for a scientific study. Initially, nineteen women and their daughters volunteered. However, after being examined, 18 pairs were immediately rejected. "In the single remaining case a "Mrs. Alpha and daughter," there was apparent genetic identity in blood groups and several other genetically determined traits including electrophoretic analysis of serum. The probability of such a close match between a mother and daughter produced by heterosexual reproduction was less than one chance in a hundred (P < .01). As a final check, reciprocal skin grafts were carried out. The transplant from daughter to mother was rejected (shed) in about 4 weeks, while the one from mother to daughter remained healthy for 6 weeks before it was removed. Balfour-Lynn (1956) considered these skin graft results obscure… autoimmune responses are known that result in rejection of grafts of one's own skin. Clearly, the jury is still out on this intriguing question: further studies like this one should be undertaken. By now, "Mrs. Alpha's daughter" may well have daughters of her own that could be tested by modern techniques such as DNA fingerprinting."

quantum physics:

> Two particles can become 'entangled' in such a way that the state of one instantly impacts the other, no matter the distance between them. It's as if they're whispering secrets across the universe!...A particle exists in all its theoretical states simultaneously until observed. [Schrodinger's Famous Cat] thought experiment posits a cat that is both alive and dead, till we check. It's the universe's ultimate cliffhanger. [Furthermore] particles can sometimes do the impossible! They can pass through barriers, seemingly like magic, thanks to their wave-like properties. It's like walking into a locked room and suddenly finding yourself on the other side.[1]

Those of you who remember your basic physics will know that an atom has a nucleus surrounded by orbiting electrons. In-between is empty space. So theoretically your hand (consisting of atoms) should be able to pass through a solid table (also consisting of atoms) because of the empty spaces. You can't actually do this because of atomic forces pulling the atoms together to form something solid. If these forces were absent, even for a second, you could walk through a wall.

As for the resurrection, this is tough to rationalise. Undoubtedly, there was an empty tomb. The authorities guarding the tomb were goaded to produce the body, which at a stroke would have killed off this 'lie,' but they didn't. Then the disciples claimed to have

---

[1] https://stanislavkondrashov.com/stanislav-kondrashov-blog/the-mysteries-of-quantum-physics/

seen and ate with Jesus on several occasions. He was also seen by over five hundred people at the same time. If it was all a lie, then how could twelve illiterate nobodies (40% of whom were fishermen) who had previously hidden themselves in order to avoid arrests, turn their cowardice into martyrdom and develop a new faith which would become the dominant one in the Roman Empire within a hundred years? They were followers of a poor carpenter from northern Israel, and had no money, influence, power, or social media! They did not have an army to conquer lands and impose their faith. Furthermore, they were foreigners from a tiny part of Israel who couldn't impose their beliefs and practices on Imperial Rome without being brutally persecuted. It all seems highly improbable, and yet it happened. Incidentally, if the disciples wanted to fabricate the greatest lie in history about the resurrection, they would not have used women as their key witnesses. Why? Because women in the first century were inferior 'persona non grata' meaning they could not testify in a court of law. In the male chauvinistic society, some pharisees would not even speak or look at a woman in public. There was a group called the 'bruised and bleeding pharisees' who, every time they saw a woman in public would close their eyes and walk into walls! Such was the status of women then. Even Jesus' disciples did not believe the women initially. So no one 'inventing' the resurrection would have concocted the story with women as the key witnesses.

For me, the resurrection can only be explained by the divinity of Jesus. In the material world, matter is indestructible. It can change its form (ice, water, vapour), but matter remains. So perhaps, upon death, our bodily molecules may be re-assembled, like a pupa turning into a butterfly. It remains mysterious, just like much of quantum physics, but not wholly irrational.

But I Am Not Religious

Neither am I. And who said anything about religion anyway? There is a difference between religion and Christianity – religion is about rules and Christianity is about a relationship. It is about coming into a relationship with your Creator and getting to know him as a heavenly father. Christianity at its best, calls people to higher things – beyond selfishness and materialism, towards love for others and the pursuit of justice, all flowing from a relationship with the Creator. By the way, the early followers of Jesus were called disciples and their new faith was initially called "The Way." The word "Christian" was a nickname which just happened to stick. I bet you didn't know that.

There are many ecclesiastical barriers to belief. I suffered from them once. The German pastor, anti-Nazi dissident and martyr, Dietrich Bonhoeffer was so disillusioned with the church's support of Hitler that he longed for a 'church without religion'. And yes, the church is full of hypocrites, but as I've said earlier, there is always room for one more. Being a Christian does not mean that you are good or superior or suddenly religious. It just means that you want to live in God's world in God's way. Christians are people who know they cannot rid themselves of their moral cancer and who accept that God is the only one who can 'cure' them. They are terminally sick people slowly being made well again. They are not religious. They are just people who are happy – grateful that they have been made well.

We said earlier that radio waves are passing through you right now but you would never know it unless you turn on your radio. In a similar way, God is beaming out signals to us all the time. We can only get in touch by tuning our 'radios' on.

We live in a universe of incredible beauty as well as suffering. The incredible sight of the galaxies of stars in the night sky of Southern Africa simply takes your breath away. But the ugliness of the suffering in Auschwitz, Rwanda, or Darfur and children dying from hunger and war, it makes one sick with indignation. In the face of this, many have often felt that the only God they can believe in is someone who knows firsthand what it is like to experience hell on earth. What about all this stuff about heaven and hell? Simply put, decisions form character. The difference between Hitler and Mother Teresa started somewhere with a small decision. Heaven and Hell is just the externalisation of our character.

Final Word Or Two...

As you will appreciate, this is my personal rational explanation for my faith. Am I absolutely convinced? NO. Sometimes doubt still creeps in, especially when I see suffering like mindless killing, children sold into human trafficking, or the wholesale destruction of forests which kills all the wildlife. For me, the journey to faith is a 'long and winding road'. But doubt is healthy. It forces me to re-think my assumptions and prejudices. All of us have unfounded presuppositions that we believe in, regardless of the facts. It is called 'implicit bias'. It is healthy to challenge our implicit bias at regular intervals so that we live what Socrates called 'an examined life.'

We all have a worldview formed from birth and by our families, friends, and culture. Mine changed from a polytheistic one (though I am pleased it was the goddess of mercy that my family followed, rather than any of the terrifying looking gods) to an atheistic one, believing in the science of evolution. Changing my worldview to a theistic one has allowed me to fit various pieces together into a more coherent and satisfying framework that is more consistent with reality.

We know that even single cells like an amoeba or a DNA has 'purpose' (scientists call it 'directionality'!). Humans also have purpose, sometimes projecting forward into decades. We have all at times wondered about the purpose of life, the universe and everything else. Can a universe that came about by chance, without a purpose, result in humans with purpose? We are all on a quest to understand what it means to be human, what it means to be here on this tiny speck of earth among the stars, with eternal yearnings in our hearts. This too has led me to believe that a theistic worldview might be more consistent with our experience of life.

Is the Christian story believable and plausible? Maybe. Certainly, it's not totally irrational. Do I still have moments of doubt? Sure. But when I stand on top of a hill and look at the beauty around me or watch the sun set over the ocean in Cape Town, something of the wonder and beauty pierces my heart and I inch closer to the Creator of it all. Like Louis Armstrong sang: "and I think to myself, what a wonderful world" created by a wonderful God.

Bibliography

Al-Khalili, J 'The World According to Physics' (Princeton University Press)

Clegg, B '30-second Quantum Theory' (Icon Books UK)

Kondrashov, S 'The mysteries of Quantum Physics' (Stanislav Kondtashov Official Website)

Forster & Marston, Reason & Faith (Monarch)

Lewis, CS 'Mere Christianity' (HarperCollins)

Collins, F 'The Language of God' (Simon & Schuster)

Dawkins, R 'The God Delusion' (Houghton Mifflin)

McGrath, 'Deluded About God? A reflection on Richard Dawkins' The God Delusion'(CS Lewis Institute)

Bruce, FF 'The New Testament Documents: Are they Reliable? (Kingsley Books)

Sire, J 'The Universe Next Door' (Intervarsity Press)

Lennox, J 'God's Undertaker: Has Science Buried God?' (Lion Books)

Appendix

The following article is taken from The Telegraph.

https://www.telegraph.co.uk/news/2023/12/25/moses-parting-red-sea-no-miracle-meteorological-phenomena/

Moses' Parting of the Red Sea May Not Have Been A Miracle After All

Meteorological phenomena could be behind the parting of the Red Sea, which allowed Moses to help the Israelites escape the Egyptians, a study suggests.

Rebekah Garratt and Rikesh Kunverji, students from the University of Leicester's School of Biological Sciences, argue there were four natural occurrences which could account for the drying of the area.

Negative surges, eastern winds, tidal surges and Rossby Waves, may have caused a resurgence of water large enough to enable a crossing on foot.

Writing in the Journal of Interdisciplinary Topics, the pair conclude: "Investigating into the methods in which the waters may have receded, allowing Moses to cross safely, may be dependent on having 'perfect' conditions, but are still physically feasible events.

"Meteorological phenomena are known to be notoriously unpredictable and can lead to chaotic chains of events leading to extreme phenomena, which may have been viewed by bystanders as the 'parting of the sea'.

"Whether a miraculous act of God or due to some of the unlikely, coincidental phenomena discussed in this paper, the chance of 'parting' is not zero."

How it may have happened

The parting of the Red Sea appears in the Book of Exodus, which describes how Moses: "...stretched out his hand over the sea; and the Lord caused the sea to go back by a strong east wind all that night and made the sea into dry land, and the waters were divided".

The Leicester team said that a phenomenon called "wind setdown" in which a particularly strong and persistent wind can lower water levels in one area while causing water to build up downwind.

Wind setdowns, which are the opposite of storm surges, have been widely documented, including in the Nile delta in the 19th century when a powerful wind pushed away about five feet of water and exposed dry land.

The team said the wind speed would need to be "considerable" to have kept the water apart for an extended period.

A second possibility is that stronger-than-normal spring tides coupled with windy conditions, could have allowed water levels to drop to such an extent that a drying area was formed, allowing the Israelites to cross.

Many believe that the Gulf of Suez would be the best location for Moses to have crossed because it is known for its large tidal fluctuations.

The team write: "Tidal resonance occurs when a sudden, unexpected external input, such as extreme wind, excites one of the resonant modes of a local region of the Red Sea, leading to a much more extreme low tide, exposing greater areas of the seabed."

Napoleon almost caught out

The phenomenon is thought to be how Napoleon and his army crossed the Red Sea in 1789.

Louis-Antoine Fauvelet de Bourrienne, Napoleon's private secretary wrote: "On the morning of the 28th we crossed the Red Sea dry shod... Near the port the Red Sea is not above 1,500 metres wide, and is always fordable at low water... at high tide the water rises five or six feet at Suez, and when the wind blows fresh it often rises nine or ten feet."

Napoleon - like the Egyptians - was almost caught out by the rising tide and drowned.

Printed in Dunstable, United Kingdom